Affectionate Moon

Passionate Reflections

By Juliette Moon

Copyright © 2004 by Juliette Moon

ISBN 0-7414-2011-2

Published by:

PUBLISHING.COM

1094 New Dehaven Street, Suite 100
West Conshohocken, PA 19428-2713
Info@buybooksontheweb.com
www.buybooksontheweb.com
Toll-free (877) BUY BOOK
Local Phone (610) 941-9999
Fax (610) 941-9959

Printed in the United States of America

Printed on Recycled Paper

Published August 2004

Introduction

Affectionate Moon is inspired by experiences, observations and dreams. The reflections are intense and captivating. The intensity of each poem takes you on a journey each time you read. They provide you the opportunity to experience tenderness and passion; they disguise hidden secrets and desires; and they invite you to indulge in substance, sensuality and reality. During your voyage, witness an outpour of emotions: humor, protests, fantasies and humiliation. Relax and reflect and realize that you are not alone in your journey. I will be your tour guide. But I must caution that you may encounter turbulence or extreme heat.

Dedication

Beatrice Moon taught me humility and integrity. I learned how to cry when I felt pain; to certainly say, "I'm sorry" when I've done wrong; to acknowledge other peoples' feelings; to evaluate myself; and to love unconditionally. Beatrice is my Mother. She rests in peace. I teach KiKi to love and give unselfishly; to say when she is unable to accomplish tasks; and to live in self-harmony. Lekisia (KiKi) is my Daughter. On June 12, 1994, Lekisia told me, "Mother, Thank you for my life." She was 2 days shy of three-years-old. The joy I encountered is etched in my heart and soul. For these reasons, I dedicate this book to my two favorite bookends.

Acknowledgments

I submit my utmost thanks to educators who are responsible for my personal and professional growth. Thanks to individuals who have contributed to the implementation and distribution of this book, including my friends. You are the ingredients for my recipes. Without you, I am not able to wet anyone's appetite. My absolute Thanks go to my Spiritual Order. You encompass all that I acknowledge. Thank you so much for making me a woman who cherishes children and fully respects the elderly.

Table of Contents

YOU'RE NOT ALONE

You're not alone when you feel pain.

I can feel it too.

You're not alone when skies are dreary and

you'll never know when they'll be blue.

You're not alone when you've experienced

hurt like never before.

You're not alone when you feel you'll never love

anymore.

You're not alone when your heart is torn and

you wish that it would mend.

You're not alone when you have lost that very

special friend.

You're not alone when a new love is definitely

hard to find.

You're not alone when you settle for someone

against your better judgment and they turn out

to be jealous and unkind.

You're not alone when trust is gone and hope
will soon follow.

You're not alone when you feel like there's no
tomorrow.

You're not alone when times are hard and you're
feeling bad.

You're not alone when you refuse to love but
you wish you had.

You're not alone when you feel that you're rejected.

God restores your faith.

He won't leave you unprotected.

Just hear what God has to say. He provides you with
subtle hints and warnings. He shows you a sign that
you deny.

When things go wrong, we play the victim and we ask
God, "Why?"

You're not alone when you've lost hope and faith.

You're not alone in your journey.

I've traveled that road too.

OUR NATION'S HEART

You are here for our Nation's spiritual eyes to see.

You are here in our hearts.

Your breath of life has been set free.

You left us at a time we would never expect.

It was a time to take your journey.

Your directions have been set.

Twin Towers stood beautifully against the New York skies.

The World had undying support and you're the reason why.

Being culturally diverse, you fulfilled International dreams.

World Trade was your specialty.

You worked in close knit teams.

Your Towers are no more but they leave a legacy.

Tuesday, September 11, 2001 made history.

The Nation was touched.

The World continues to mourn.

You left families, friends,

and babies who would be born.

The Nation will never forget the families, friends and

colleagues who were touched by your untimely plight.

God embodied you and gave you wings to take flight.

We will cherish the many heroes in the air, on the

waters and those on the ground.

You spared lives and protected us from the

terror we were unable to see.

You risked your lives to save the United States from a

larger catastrophe.

Even though you rushed to the scene, it was worse

than it appeared.

We watched television in shock and horror.

Our eyes were filled with tears.

Your intrepidity left us speechless.

You are etched in our Nation's heart.

We feel your love coming from the tranquil skies

above.

In our hearts you will always stay.

Every year you will be honored and remembered

in a very special way.

Thank you for our lives.

.

WITHOUT YOU ANOTHER DAY

Another day has come to an end.
I wish that my heart would only mend.
I sent you away tearing me apart.
You left out of the door.
I felt pain in my heart.
I sat and wondered throughout the day.
Why didn't you compromise?
Instead, you went away.
I felt so badly when you left out of the door.
I have this piercing feeling like never before.
As night begins to fall,
I wonder if you would call.
You left out the door with nothing to say.
I sit and wait patiently by the phone.
I'm without you another day.
I sit, endlessly, all alone waiting for your call.
Our love was so strong.
I didn't think it could fall.
All I do is cry both night and day, since you
have left and gone away.
My feelings for you are so strong.
I still sit waiting by the phone.
I sent the one I love far away.
I feel that I've been without you another day.
Please let those words erase from your mind.
I didn't love you enough.
I became very unkind.
I looked at my watch and realized that it's only
been a few minutes since you've been away.
The feeling's so strong.
I feel so alone.
I've imagined being without you another day.

IT'S DEFINITELY REAL!

Your love is so tantalizing and mesmerizing.

You know how to make me feel.

You have true love in your heart.

It's definitely real!

I am amazed by your charm.

We kid around and you then take me into your arms.

You stare into my eyes and tell me how you feel.

Your love for me is genuine.

It's definitely real!

You set no boundaries because the sky is the limit.

You tell me how much I mean to you.

I will submit my heart to yours. It was my heart that you chose to pursue.

I am not afraid to give you all of me.

I don't have to tell you what I want.

It's my heart that you can feel.

You know how to treat a woman.

It's definitely real!

I'm told that I give love like no other woman in the world.

I think your love is priceless also.

All my dreams and fantasies you do fulfill.

Your love is worth your weight in gold.

It's definitely real!

Others don't share like you and I.

We go through great times together and together we cry.

We compromise and we sacrifice.

We do selfless things for others and each other.

Our love is envied.

It's definitely real!

We both love unconditionally.

To be hurt by others, we know how it feels.

Our love is original and it can never be duplicated.

It's definitely real!

NEGLECTED GENTLENESS

He often criticizes her but she is required to submit to his expectations. While she wants to share his burdens, he wants to make love to relieve frustrations.

He does not want to make love, but lustful aggression. She allows him to do what he wants to do while she goes through depression.

All that matters to her is that she makes everything perfect for her man. He often sends her through hell and yet he doesn't understand.

Her maternal instincts are strong and she wants to bring a replica into the world. He's relentless and he doesn't want the responsibilities of a boy or a girl.

Despite going through hell, she accepts his negative attitude. She makes so many concessions for him and he shows her no gratitude.

He creates so many problems. She is forbidden to discuss them. He feels that they are strictly her issues and he refuses to resolve them.

He definitely feels that he is a man when he can relate to the negative things that his friends can do.

He's so deceitful but his friends mislead him and tell him that he's true.

Don't let her be honest and tell him about his "true self." He'll call her crazy, make her feel worthless, and tell her about "herself."

She actually thinks that something is wrong with her. She believes what he says. She then realizes that he's insecure and he tries to hide it in so many ways.

She becomes fed up with his trifling attitude and she begins to retaliate. She should have done something sooner because it may be too late.

She takes no more abuse but she's called every name in the world. He does not want her to be a woman, but a "powerless little girl."

She'll be cordial with him and take things one-step at a time. He becomes suspicious and accuses her of sleeping with another man and he may commit a crime.

It may be a crime of passion or a different crime. She'll forgive him and choose not to press charges. He may serve no time.

All she wants is for him to be the man he "proclaims" to be. He makes poor excuses, makes her look bad and says, "You can't change me!"

He'll do everything possible to get what he wants as long as he's "respected." It does not matter if she's the mother of his child, his wife, his own Mother or even the woman next door. Even though she's gentle and yet she's neglected.

Your Exclusive Sax

Oh my jazzman.
You play to the bone.
I'm your most favorite fan.

I'm your exclusive saxophone.

You could have chosen any other wind instrument.
You could have even chosen the xylophone.
But you chose me exclusively.

I'm your saxophone!

You don't have to make a request.
I know exactly what to do.
Just hold me.
Place your lips against me.
Press firmly.
I'll do the rest for you.

When you play, it can be for a long time.
I'll do what you want.
Take your lips and press them firmly against mine.
Play me to the bone.

I'm exclusively your saxophone.

People see how well we go together.
It's a match that is priceless.

It's made for just us two.
I can hit a note that's so deep.
All you have to do is press against me.

I'll give you results that will be just for you.

Others wonder why you play so well.
You take care of me.

You play me to the bone.
Your caress is so gentle.

I'm your exclusive saxophone.

When your mouth touches me, it turns me on.
I'll swing and I'll sway as you hold me in the air.
I'll make sounds that are soothing, sultry and sassy.

Press the keys you want and I'll do the rest for you.
You can play privately, right here at home.
The sounds are meant for only us two.

I'm your exclusive saxophone!

I can feel the magic in your hands.
I can feel the tremble in your lips.
I love how you caress me with your fingertips.

I love when I'm high in the air.
You handle me with such passion.
It is with such care.

Your lips feel so good to me.
You play me aggressively.
You play me tenderly.

Oh jazz man you do what you will.
You know how to play to the bone.

That's why I'm your saxophone.

The crowd loves it when you play with such aggression!
They give us both a standing ovation.

You play remarkably well.
That's your chosen profession.

You can play one-on-one.
You can play for a large crowd.
I won't be jealous.

I know how to complement you.
You have the right touch.
You take care of me.
I definitely know what to do for you.

You can place me back in my case.
Your touch is everlasting.

I never feel alone.
You know how to stroke me well.
You're my favorite fan.

I'm your exclusive saxophone!

When I'm Unhappy

When I'm unhappy

I'm in misery.

I make sure I'm alone

and have no company.

When I'm unhappy

I make my pain my own.

I stay to myself

and leave other people alone.

When I'm unhappy

I know what I have to do for me.

I confront my issues

and face them responsibly.

I reassess and evaluate myself.

I have come to realize that

the most wonderful thing about me....

I make my misery no one's company.

Season's Best!

Ice water in the summer time.

You're still hot! You're still mine.

Watermelon

Lemonade

Iced Coffee

Iced Tea

You like Kool-aid. But you love me!

Hot Chocolate

Hot Coffee

Hot Tea

Fall is here. You're still with me.

Soup

Chili

Homemade Pastries

Your love is sweet.

Your kisses are tasty.

Snowballs

Slush

Angel Soft Snow

Whenever I need you, you remain my hero!

The winter air is cold and bitter.

Your heart is warm!

Your smile just glitters.

Winter is leaving

and turning into spring.

The flowers bloom

and the birds sing.

Your love is the season's best.

It withstands the elements.

That's the biggest test.

The Fragile Doorstep

The child who never asked to come into the world

is the innocent baby boy and baby girl.

The soft and fragile tissue born is so innocently

placed in a secret spot for no one else to see.

It has no idea of how it was conceived.

It has no idea of how it will survive.

It's a beautiful being who arrives here dead

or sometimes born alive.

There are some babies who never make it even

though they were born.

They are left for other people to feel the pain and

mourn.

The little one is left where it can be missed.

Some are left just anywhere.

This tiny little angel is so helpless and hungry.

The baby has the ability to let someone know that it

does exist.

But they have no control over their fate.

Maybe the precious one will be found in time.

Sometimes the doorbell can be too late.

The hospital is the best place for an unwanted child.

It would make a wonderful gift for parents who are

unable to have children.

They have adoption in mind and they can hardly wait.

Please remember that you were once helpless babies.

Taking the child to a warm and safe environment is

absolutely your responsibility.

Place *yourself* in that baby's blanket.

Can you imagine how it would feel to have

someone throw you away against your will?

Nature

Ants can crawl. Birds can fly.
Nothing matters but you and I.
Groundhogs hide. Monkeys play.
I think of you both night and day.

Horses gallop. Lions roar.
I love you like never before.
I have loved you right from the start.
You're etched in my mind.
I'll always hold you in my heart.

You look wonderful with grace and style.
I love your wit. I love your smile.
Nothing can be more natural
than what we have acquired.
Making me your only love
is what I have always admired.

Our hearts are unified with
love weighing a ton.
As long as nature exists,
we'll always remain as one!

Flowers are beautiful.
The rain falls fast.
Your love for me was made to last.
I am part of you.
You are part of me.
Our love will last infinitely.

Another Day Without Your Love

Another day has come to an end.

I haven't felt your touch.

I don't remember when.

All those unkind words just tore us apart.

You left out the door leaving pain in my heart.

I was bothered by you having nothing to say.

I'm without your love for another day.

I've felt this void since you left out the door.

The pain in my heart is like never before.

I sit waiting endlessly watching the phone.

Don't make excuses to leave me alone.

It's only been a few minutes since you've gone
away.

But the feelings are so strong.

I feel all alone.

I feel I'm without your love for another day.

Bible Interpretation

I am unable to interpret the Bible when it's read.
But I *understand* clearly when the words are being
said.

I don't sit in a church every Sunday to listen to
someone preach. I learn the Lord's word *everywhere*.
For it's myself that I *must* spiritually teach.

I do *realize* that it's his word that I must know.
It's others who *assist* me and make it so.
I give money that I'm able to afford.
I give selflessly because I am lead by the Lord.

I give to others *who need* help immediately.
I'm a steward not just on Sundays but *all* of the time.
I donate to schools, churches, charitable organizations
and I give to the homeless, *especially*.

They are not just individuals sleeping and panhandling
on the street.
But the homeless are also *innocent* children who
occupy a seat.

I'm committed to them because that is where I have
been *lead*.
I teach them life skills, social issues and I help them
to *interpret* what is being read.

We read the Bible for many reasons, especially to
interpret and follow God's word.
For students who are unable to read and/or write, the
Bible is also a *tool* that is being heard.

MOUTH-WATERING CHOCOLATE

I never personally met the finest chocolate in the land.
He's the type of chocolate that can melt in your hand.

I am very *particular* about the chocolate that I choose.
With this fine ass chocolate, you can't lose.

Some women refer to men as a type of shoe.
I Choose to refer to them as types of chocolate.
Allow me to advertise for you.

There are hundreds of the finest chocolates that
come in different flavors.
Some are very bitter, too sweet, too nutty,
too hard or chewy.
Some are semisweet, crunchy, soft, and
some are too gooey.

I wanted to sample that fine dark milk chocolate
for a long time.
I know how to savor the flavor.
I wanted to make that chocolate mine.

I had a profound crush on Mr. fine ass milk chocolate.
He did notice me,
but he had a chocolate brother
who was crunchy.
He pursed me aggressively.

His crunchy ass made it a point to pursue what he
wanted.
His infatuation was deep and definitely undaunted.

I never got a chance to tell Mr. chocolate bar how I felt.
You could look at him and just simply melt.

He knows not of my current existence
because he moved from Chicago many years ago.
I think he would have allowed me to have him,
if I just let him know.

I was not attracted to his fine ass, of course.
I was drawn to his intelligent and athletic source.

He was the perfect officer and gentleman
you would ever want to see.
I would have submitted to him if he first noticed me.

His name is Jackie and that is all I have to say.
He may be happily married
and I want to keep it that way.

I would never want to invade
someone else's chocolate.
I want the same respect.
I dreamed about him for many years.
He is the finest mouth-watering
milk chocolate that I'll never forget!

Ki Ki

She was two days
shy of three-years-old when
she said,
"Mother, Thank-you for my life."
Three miscarriages sent me through a lot of
pain and strife.
She knows that she is my joy.
I am a very grateful Mother.
She manages perfectly well
without a Sister or a Brother.
I will never forget the time
when she tried to tie her shoe.
Despite how many times I showed her,
she forgot what to do.
I was downstairs getting ready for work.
She was at the top of the landing
when I heard her say, "Damn!"
She was fussing with her shoe.
A snapshot could not capture that special
moment.
I wished I had the cam.
The remarkable things she says
will have you rolling on the floor.
Just listen to what she says.
You'd think she's been here before.

Promotion Criterion

Just sleep with me.
You don't have to be my woman,
nor I your man.
You want something from me.
I need something from you.
I hope you understand.

It doesn't matter if you deserve a promotion.
I want you to have it rather fast.
Let me touch your thighs while no one's looking.
I want the feeling to last.

I realize that I sound selfish.
But you need something from me.
You can get it by taking care of my sexual
fantasy.

I know that you feel cheap and humiliated.
That's the way it has to be.
I got where I am today by giving in
to women who were certainly horny.

You may think that my rationale sounds lame.
Research and see how many people, in all
professions, play the job promotion game.

Daughter To Father

Dear Daddy:

I saw you on the corner although we've never met.
Mom showed me a picture of you, a face I'll never
forget.

I observed you talking to a girl holding a bottle in your
hand.
Mom told me that I have 10 other brothers and sisters.
I just don't understand.

I met a young man who acts just like you.
He painted a beautiful portrait of himself.
He says that he likes only me. I know it isn't true.

I see him talking to other girls, trying to get them in bed.
He'll place his hands around their waists and deceitfully
fill their heads.

Mom told me that she loved you.
You were a man with a wealth of knowledge.
She said that you could have been a scholar and easily
made it through college.

Now I see a homeless person who could have made a
difference in the world. You preferred to sleep from
house-to-house with just any girl.

I am tired of men and women making senseless
excuses. When you bring us into the world without any
goals. It is simply useless.

We try to emulate things that our parents do.
You are my Father, but I just can't follow you.

You've set a poor example for all the children
you brought into the world.
That's why we have so many bitter boys and girls.

But Mom is the best thing that has ever happened to
us. Being both parents to us has been a challenge, but
her goals have been met.
Our college tuition is paid in full. Our goals have been
set.

Daddy, I love you.

You helped to bring me into the world.
I hold no grudges.

Take care.

Sincerely,

Your little girl.

When You Cry For That Man

Make sure he *served* our Country well and not jail time.

Make sure he has *committed* a selfless act and not a crime.

Make sure it is a criminal that he *attacks* and not an innocent victim whose car he jacks.

Make sure it was a large vocabulary that he *stole* and not someone's material possessions.

Make sure he *professed* his love *for God* and he made interminable confessions.

Make sure his *drugs* are God's words and not the substances that make him fly like a bird.

Make sure the alcohol he drinks is *large* amounts of water that cleanses his soul and not the fluids that destroy his liver.

Make sure he is not a taker, but a light-hearted giver.

Make sure he's spiritual and fights for God's purpose and not for the thuggish gang.

Make sure his words are of encouragement and not language that is vulgar or profane.

Make sure he is a man of *integrity* and not one who tries to destroy other people's lives.

Make sure he is a *strong* man who maintains and curtails other men's mates or wives.

Make sure you receive from him the utmost respect.

Make sure he has a job that he won't fret.

Make sure when he *embraces* you he is very affectionate,
and not enraged with jealousy that is passionate.

Make sure he *controls* his own destiny
and not a woman's mind.

Make sure he realizes that he's not *invincible*
but humble and sublime.

Make sure you're not blinded by his charm but you can
see how he has committed to God and he realizes that
any day he can die.

Make sure you are a strong and resilient woman
who uses *discretion* when you cry.

My Favorite Men's Cologne

The sensual flavor turns me on.
It's my aromatherapy.
The man who wears it
will have a wonderful time with me.
The kinds I like are a secret to treasure.
The love I make will be his pleasure.
He can't just wear that cologne,
but he must also do what's right.
Touch me in my most sensitive places
and I can make love all night.
He doesn't have to work hard and long, just
occasionally.
He can never be one who lacks affection.
Foreplay must be his forte and his chosen
profession.
"Hitting and quitting it"
is a riddle I could never solve.
The secret is not in the strokes.
Strokes can be useless.
Any ordinary man can stroke you.
The secret is in body movements and the power
of the hand.
Cologne is really next to what turns me on.
The man must be shower-fresh and breath
smelling like mint.
I take care of business.
My body is clean and fresh
with a mouth-watering scent.
I prefer a man who is a gentleman.
With him, I can't go wrong.
I enjoy sharing gentle passion
with a man who has on stimulating cologne.

Now That You're a Father

Now that you're a Father and you've
become a man, do you still think that
parents simply don't understand?
You have a young son now.
It's definitely true.
Do you allow him to do
what he actually wants to do?
Are you apprehensive about telling him
what's right and what's wrong?
Do you let him know where the line is drawn?
Do you tell him that kids can't have
everything they want while keeping in mind that
children rebel?
Do you think about a child's protests, temper-
tantrums, and physical violence landing them in
reform school or jail?
Do you think about children hitting their siblings
and some hitting their parents too?
Do you think parents don't understand when
they were once young like you?
Can you think back and remember when you
were bad?
Do you now wish that you had the will and
strength that your own parents had?
Will you allow your son to make choices
while keeping in mind what may
be best for a young man?
Now that you are an experienced Father,
do you still think that parents just don't
understand?

Likes Really Attract

"Opposites attract-Likes repel"
only in physical science.

A successful relationship can be
a genuine and wonderful alliance.

No matter the physical
and/or mental attraction,
a match can be made in heaven or
It can be one straight from hell.

Personal corruption
and lack of discretion
and communication
make relationships repel.

Lies and deception
stand in the way
of successful romances.

Sometimes in life we don't care to start over
and take more chances.

No matter the sexual preference,
the results are based on chance.

Likes and opposites will either
succeed or fail at romance.

A *Romantic* Recipe

Take two loving people
to make special recipes.

They are affectionate playmates
who have license to please.

The following ingredients you should mix:
Greet your mate at the door daily with a kiss.

Make sure the lines of communication are open
everyday.

Talk and listen to each other and respect what
both have to say.

Never compare the past relationships to what
you have now.

Growing and maturing together makes you
understand how.

Surprise each other with just-because notes and
a special treat.

Give back massages, body basting in lotions
or oils and rub the feet.

Go on trips together
Take romantic walks in the park.
Wish upon a star together
when it's long after dark.

Make everyday special
and leave room for errors and mistakes.

Maintain honesty and compliment each other
and do what it takes
to make each other laugh
and embrace each other
during trying times.
Respect each other's differences
and always compromise.

Take a loving home
and mix all of the ingredients carefully.
This recipe is priceless
and it can be made successfully.

Carefully put in understanding,
forgiveness, affection, happiness,
communication and protection.

This kind of recipe is too strong
to cut with a knife.
They say it's variety,
but romance is the spice of life.

Romance makes this recipe
a delightful pleasure.
It is full of herbs and spices
that one can never measure.

BADD AZZ KIDZ

Those badd azz kidz:
- [ ] Will lift your wallet and steal your purse.
- [ ] Don't have to be pissed-off for them to curse.
- [ ] Get in a bunch then they attack.
- [ ] See cars they want and then jack.
- [ ] Won't study in school and want to cheat.
- [ ] Ignore the elderly who need a seat.
- [ ] Will smash windows for a quick grab.
- [ ] Leave the restaurants and skip the tab.
- [ ] Will taunt a couple on a date.
- [ ] Will criticize others they may hate.
- [ ] Will steal the clothes off of your back.
- [ ] Can't keep a job because they slack.
- [ ] Are too scared to fight without a weapon.
- [ ] Use others as a rug for them to step on.
- [ ] Will keep a straight face and tell a lie.
- [ ] Question their honesty, they wonder why.
- [ ] Drink alcohol while taking drugs.
- [ ] Glorify gang activity and cherish thugs.
- [ ] Will have sex with several people in one day.
- [ ] Will use persuasion to get their way.
- [ ] Become suspicious and turn on each other.
- [ ] Have no respect for Father and none for Mother.
- [ ] Use pitiful excuses to do wrongs.
- [ ] End up rapping gang-related songs.

Repeat offenders with feelings that can't be felt,
inevitably become Badd Azz Adultz!

Educated Bitch!

She has valuable time for her books

Will glance at a man without second looks

Tries to balance her books, work and a man

He envies school and doesn't understand

The hours she shares are not enough

He conjures up a scheme and gets tough

He says that her books come before he does

The books were there before he was

He doesn't realize that she's trying to grow

He threatens to move on and let her go

She displays little reaction to his protest

She makes her decision and does what's best

She tried to share her time but he had no time

for her

He chose to be where other women were

He played a game for her to choose

She politely spelled out to him "you lose!"

When access was denied inside her door, he called her an educated bitch!

He couldn't accept her denying him and simply making a switch.

He never denied her being educated.

Love was never in his heart.

He was lustful and simply infatuated.

He failed to realize that she was the perfect one.

Her website is www.educatedbitch!.com.

She enjoys being **B**eautiful, **I**ntriguing, **T**alented, **C**harismatic and **H**appy!

His negative perception of her facilitated in building her character. It made her twice as strong.

His condemnation actually showed her just where she stood with him and where he belongs.

MY AMERICAN EXPERIENCE

Making a world of difference for us.
Yielding to those who serve our country with trust

Aiming for our country to be the best it can be.
Making endless opportunities for you and for me.
Entertaining cultures from many places.
Responsible for a world of happy faces.
International dreams fulfilled right here.
Courage is worn by our troops with barely a tear.
Atmospheric pressure displaying our flag at its best.
Never placing us in office, combat, or orbit without a
test.

Empowering our country to stand at its highest peak.
Xeroxing success without appearing mystique.
Protecting us from eminent dangers and harms.
Entering the waters with books/torch held in her arms.
Reaching for the skies over the waters.
Informing all of its sons and its daughters.
Educating and enlightening us on its political views.
Never forgetting its patriotic morals and values.
Care and respect for its young and old.
Enunciated history with many success stories untold.

A WOMAN'S RIGHTS

A WOMAN'S RIGHTS DOES NOT MEAN BEING BETTER THAN
A MAN. IT SIMPLY MEANS THAT MEN SHOULD TAKE NOTE
AND UNDERSTAND, THAT WE ARE QUALIFIED, GIFTED AND
TRUE WITHOUT YOU CONTROLLING WHAT WE SAY AND DO.

WE CAN PERFORM A JOB WITH PROFICIENCY.
HAVE A RELATIONSHIP AND MAINTAIN INDIVIDUALITY.
WE NEED FOR YOU TO COMPLEMENT US. BE OUR
MATCHING BOOKEND WITHOUT A FUSS.

YOU MAKE A GAME OUT OF WOMEN'S RIGHTS. MAKING
PEOPLE END UP IN VIOLENT FIGHTS. TURNING THE TRUTH
INTO GROSS DISTORTIONS. DENYING THE CHILD, INSISTING
ON ABORTIONS.

YOU TRIED TO TAKE AWAY OUR EXISTENCE AS MUCH AS
YOU COULD. NOT GIVING US THE RESPECT THAT YOU
SHOULD. WHEN YOUR LIBIDO NEEDS STIMULATING, YOU
FIND THE TIME. WHEN WE TAKE CHARGE, YOU MAKE IT A
CRIME.

YOU GIVE US LITTLE POWER AND NOT MUCH MORE,
WHILE NEEDING US LIKE NEVER BEFORE. IT IS A WOMAN
FROM WHOM YOU CAME. IT IS SHE WHO SHARED IN GIVING
YOU YOUR BIRTH NAME.

THE PILLAR OF STRENGTH, YOU WOULD NEVER ADMIT.
WHEN A WOMAN PERFORMS WELL, YOU HAVE A FIT.
YOU SAY THAT THIS JOB IS MADE FOR A MAN. BUT WHEN
WE PERFORM IT WITH PROFICIENCY, YOU COULD NEVER
UNDERSTAND.

YOU ALSO SAY THAT YOU ARE THE STRONGER SEX.
YOU PUT UP YOUR MUSCLES AND THEN YOU FLEX.
STRENGTH IS NOT ONLY WHAT YOU SHOW. IT IS ALSO

WHAT YOU MORALLY BELIEVE IN AND SPIRITUALLY KNOW.

WE CAN BE PRESIDENT OF THE UNITED STATES.
YOU PREFER TO LOOK SUPERIOR AND PROCEED TO HATE.

YOU FEEL THAT YOU ARE THE ONLY ONE IN AUTHORITY.
YOU LIMIT OUR SUCCESS AND MAKE US SEE THAT YOU'RE
LACKING FAITH, STRENGTH AND SELF ESTEEM.
YOU ARE UNTOUCHABLE AND INVINCIBLE, SO IT SEEMS.

IF YOU ARE THE MAN THAT YOU PROCLAIM, STAND UP AND
HONESTLY TAKE THE BLAME. WHEN YOU HAVE COMMITTED
A DOMESTIC CRIME, BLAME ONLY YOURSELF AND SERVE
THE TIME. DON'T INVOLVE ME IN GAMES OF DISPLEASURE.
INCLUDE ME IN SUCCESS THAT I CAN TREASURE.

WOMEN ARE GROSSLY MISUNDERSTOOD. SINCE YOU
TREAT US THE WAY YOU DO, DISCREDITING US WHILE
REAPING THE REWARDS, WOULD YOU WEAR OUR SHOES IF
YOU HAD TO?

EQUAL RIGHTS ARE IMPORTANT FOR EVERYONE.
TAKE THEM SERIOUSLY. A MAN, WHO IS FREE OF
PREJUDICE, HAS NEVER DEFINED A WOMAN'S BEING OR
IDENTITY.

HE REALIZES HER WORTH AND VALOR
WITHOUT FEELING INHIBITED. HE SEES THAT SHE HAS A
STRAIGHT HEAD. LIKE ANGLES, THEY COMPLEMENT EACH
OTHER. HE ASKS HER FOR ASSISTANCE AND RESPECTS
HER INPUT. HE DOESN'T SEE HER BEING HIS EQUAL ONLY
IN BED.

A MAN NEVER STOOD IN THE WORLD ALONE.
HE CAN NEVER MAKE THIS WORLD HIS OWN
AND SAY THAT IT IS NOTHING WITHOUT A WOMAN
WHO BLED, PERSPIRED, AND CRIED BUILDING THIS WORLD.
THAT WOMAN EMERGED FROM A LITTLE GIRL.

REASSESS YOUR THOUGHTS AND TAKE THE TIME TO UNDERSTAND.
A WOMAN'S RIGHTS TAKE NOTHING FROM A MAN.

A Healthy Smile

When I am responsible for another parent's child

I greet him/her with a healthy smile

I am a parent who loves to teach

It's the child's heart I first must reach

That inner beauty is what I want to see

The willingness to learn is what touches me

My students learn without hesitation

I must first make evident motivation

I must show a willingness to learn

It is the student's trust that I must earn

The child can either learn or resent being there

A teacher must demonstrate faith and care

I must allow my students to make choices

I must hear their beautiful voices

I never force them to be mute

I allow them to communicate and become astute

The most important thing that I do see

is the child who learns and teaches me

When greeting them and displaying that big healthy

smile, I've touched each student's learning style

A child should never be forced to learn

He/she has innate abilities that will emerge

His/her motivation and abilities will trickle out

and sometimes they will upsurge

Allow him/her to emerge from the cocoon

and eventually become a beautiful butterfly

No two are the same

Not even you and I

Everyday I greet a student with a healthy smile

I live with a beautiful student who

happens to be my child

Excuses To Cheat

Don't make excuses to stay out late.

So what if you have an engagement that can't wait.

I won't ask what are you doing tonight.

I'll just do what I think is right.

I figure that if you wanted me to know,

you would have simply told me so.

But! That's too much for you to do.

You honestly don't know what it means to be true.

I won't be mad at you telling me the truth.

I thought I had a man, not an immature youth.

I want the same respect that I give.

You can play away from me and live.

Don't make excuses to leave me.

Just Go!

Our relationship is not written in stone.

While I'm a woman to you,

I can do without a man who does wrong.

I don't want to be in a relationship

that is only sexually defined.

I can sleep with anyone just by design.

Life's simply too short to be with anyone you please.

You're playing Russian Roulette with a disease.

My view on life stands as it is!

I don't like sharing men and body fluids.

Don't make excuses to be a man.

Just learn!

Successful relationships are

mature, defined, honest and earned.

Finding an outlet to be childish is quite useless.

Don't be selfish by running and making excuses!

Thugs Require Love Too

No matter what they say and what they do, thugs
definitely need love too.
They do things that are forbidden.
They keep drugs and weapons safety hidden.
They attract girls with cheap talk.
They threaten people with a thug-like walk.
One alone will never be solo.
That's why they recruit,
on the down low.
They multiply in the environment
and then they explore.
They rely on weapons more and more.
They are humans, who lack respect,
guidance and direction.
They require love and understanding
without affection.
They make us all victims
personally and professionally.
They even victimize their own family.
Thugs are children who lack self-esteem
and moral character.
They come in no
specific gender or culture.

People who recruit them would be the ones
you would never suspect.
That thug could be your own child.
Don't forget!

When Ruben Won

I watched American Idol intensely
The contestants impressed me immensely

I loved them all; tall, short, big and small

I loved listening to the contestants sing
and make a great effort to perform a very
unique thing

When I first heard Ruben I was pleased
He held a beautiful smile with great ease

Ruben stood in front of bright lights
and shared his hopes and dreams with great
might

The process of elimination was to vote and
choose the contestant who hit their favorite
notes

Process of elimination was down to the wire
Clay and Ruben were left to inspire

Ryan Seacrest illustriously uttered,
"Our new American Idol is....
Ruben Studdard!"

Emotions were flowing and they were streaming
People were elated
and some were steaming

When Ruben won,

I was filled with tears of gladness
I was happy for him and relieved from the madness

He was interviewed at the end to discuss his beginning
I calmed down and Thanked God for him winning

I feel that he will proudly represent the USA
Positive words are all I heard him say

He's the southern gentleman you'd want to meet
He's from my Mom's hometown in Alabama
That is sweet!

When Ruben won,
I thought that his personality was a big factor
I can see a popular recording artist and well-known actor

It touched millions of Americans, who heard
Ruben sing the future hit song,
"Flying Without Wings"

Lost Purity of Innocence

I'm lost and I know not where to go.
I'm so confused that I will let no one know.
I cry-out on the inside and keep things hidden away.
Someone whom I trusted has turned my blue skies
gray.

You can't imagine who has invaded my privacy.
It's difficult to face this painful reality.
I would never suspect it but I've been deceived.
My story will be hard for anyone to believe.

I am the victim of an ugly attack.
The last thing I want you to do is turn your back.
The physical and emotional scars are quite clear.
I realize that it is difficult for you to believe,
but the evidence is right here.

Sexuality is not taken seriously.
People aggressively take away innocence and purity.
Your denial makes me just want to lie down and die.
Instead, I sit here in pain and secretly cry.

Millions of us are victimized and want you to see
how family, friends and strangers can strip away our
dignity. Many of us are unable to endure this painful
world.

"I'm that lost little boy.
I'm that lost little girl."

Things are not the way we wished they could be.
We need love, understanding and sensitivity.

Is it not enough that we feel guilty and ashamed?
We feel that we have no one but ourselves to blame.
We're not asking for special attention.
We realize that you want to know how things
happened, but personal invasion is too painful to
mention.

I realize that as a result of our trauma
we can make the wrong decisions in life.
Your understanding can help us get through
our physical and emotional pain and strife.
I look in the mirror and I see someone else.
Despite pain and embarrassment, I must believe in
myself.

Give me all the help that I need.
Help the one who has destroyed my childhood.
Please take heed!
Pay attention as you hear my story.
Don't turn your back on me.
Don't assume anything.
Open your mind to see.

Please listen for my silent cry.
It's when I'm not heard and I
become lost and confused.
Then I want to die.

His Impossible Mission

He can become a computer,
civil or an electrical engineer
Make sophisticated equipment
by the Craftsman or John Deer
Score a Touchdown after a huddle
Test a billion dollar space shuttle

But he is unable to empower a woman

He can design blueprints for a home
Build comfortable seats for a super dome
Be the anthropologist or archaeologist
who studies life, fossils and rocks
Use computer chips to make sophisticated locks

But he is unable to be faithful to a woman

He can design an intricate circuit board
Make sure computer memory is stored
Make fiber optics for communication
Structure companies with international affiliation

But he is unable to respect a woman

He can design a flat screen computer
and a flat screen television
Write on a grain of rice with ease and precision
Design hundreds of musical instruments
Make designer cologne with invigorating scents

But he is unable to protect a woman

He can design
precious diamonds and gemstones
Accommodate consumers
with practical and sophisticated phones
Build a playground for the child who plays
Make the interstates and highways

But he is unable to love a woman

He can design and sell vehicles custom made
Make intricate patterns on a blade
Build skyscrapers for the world to admire
Design complex equipment to put out fire

But he doesn't have time for one woman

He can make himself President
of the United States
Design fast running three-wheeled skates
Make it possible for aircraft to fly
Make a tiny object for the eye

But he's not able to honor the woman

He can operate on the brain or heart
Make a brand new battery start
Discuss local and world news
Create hip-hop, jazz, rhythm and blues

But he is unable to keep his hands off a woman

He can fight for his country in wars
Design businesses and department stores
Blow beautiful and delicate glass
Demolish a building in one blast

But he is unable to commit to a woman

He can make fine china so that we can eat
Protect our bodies with central heat
Deliver a precious child into the world
Make silly toys for boys and girls

But he chooses to challenge a woman.

He can make cameras for the telephone,
computer, water and fire.
He can determine when medicine and store-
bought goods expire
He can sing a beautiful love song
Incarcerate those who commit a wrong
Make powerful electricity
sculpture an ice castle perfectly

But he is unable to be a Father to every child he
creates.

He can preach the word of the Lord
Play the amazing harpsichord
Make an encyclopedia, a thesaurus
and dictionary for our knowledge
Award scholarships and grants for college
Protect the flower that he helped to grow

But he never thinks that he will reap what he
sows

A CALL FROM SHERRI

The telephone startled me because it was rather late
Sherri had a serious question to ask me
It was an issue that really couldn't wait

I was lying next to Carl who was fast asleep
He never heard any of my conversation
Sherri introduced herself
She asked for Julie with no hesitation

She wanted to know if she could have Carl
She felt that I was in the way
I told her that I didn't mind
but I had to have my say

I wanted her to know something
she needed to understand
Carl may be my boyfriend but I don't
fight over any man

I am the kind of woman
who respects being in a relationship
I complement a man well but we're not joined at his
hip

It does not matter how well he makes love or how well
he uses his lips
Sherri heard what I was saying
She listened very well
After I had my say,
She had something to tell

I was told that Carl really cared for me

He talked about me so much
She felt a sense of guilt
I was deeply touched

Sherri met Carl in my building the day he was visiting
me
She couldn't resist his charm
He was someone she wanted to see

Sherri said that she found
my number in Carl's billfold
My number wasn't in his wallet
I know that Sherri asked him for it
and she was told

Why was Carl with me?
Why was he there?
He was lost in himself and yet he cared
He was sweet at times
Sometimes his temper flared

He slept and never moved while I talked
on the phone
Not once did he blink
He submitted to Sherri and was not man enough to
leave me
he didn't even think

A man can hide his innermost secrets
But God reveals what he wants you to know
He wanted to make things known to me
Through Sherri God made them so

I was mature about the matter
I thanked Sherri
She had no concerns for any other woman

Her concerns were strictly pertaining to me

I politely gave up Carl as I lay next to him in bed
Sherri thanked me for speaking with her
That's all that was said

I went on to sleep after thinking about the call
Whatever energy I had in me,
that conversation took it all
Sherri wanted Carl exclusively
I knew what I had to do for me

I tried to imagine Carl's reaction
I felt the need to see
I made passionate love to Carl the next morning right
before we left
I hesitated to tell him, but I had to see for myself

I told Carl that I had a talk with Sherri
She telephoned me
He started his acting debut and said,
"Who in the fuck is she!"

I expected a negative reaction
just as I witnessed him in the car
I was very mature about the matter
I was the shining star

Carl was mad as hell
He acted as if he knew nothing of the sort
I lost all the respect I had for him
He lost all of my support

When Carl lost me, he felt pretty bad
I was not only a good woman to him
But I was that friend he never had

He ventured out to take another ride
He saw that the grass was a lot browner
on the other side

He left me a disturbing message that was
indiscriminate and not so kind
He poured out his heart and said,
"I'm going out of my fuckin mind!"

I took the tape out of my answering machine
Carl's voice was filled with rage
I relinquished the relationship
and that was the very last page

Thirty-Five Seventeen

The Skyscraper
It stood proud and tall
It was made to last

Now it is a mere memory
The wind tunnel is now a thing of the past
It used to be clean

Elevators were working
We played on them just to hear the bell
Our parents would be standing in the vestibule
with a belt to see who would tell

We could camp-out on the balcony
We kept our doors unlocked
We were not worried about gang activity,
not even a gun being cocked

Thirty-Five Seventeen had mostly two-parent families
Very few people were on public aid
Girls and boys played together
Many of us were working and getting paid

We never feared gang activity
That was very low
We felt comfortable about Breezeway
Visitors would comfortably come and go

The grass was neatly cut
Hallways smelled of pine or bleach
Any floor you visited, parents were there to teach

It was a fine place to live
We helped the elderly

They were very wise
Telling us things for our good
Making sure we were doing what we should

It was fun when we ran through the breezeway
Softball, poison box and tag were some games we
would play

Sox Park had games right down the street
The fireworks were so loud; you could feel the boom
right under your feet

Use of profane language was strictly prohibited
You'd get in big trouble if you cursed
I realized that after we moved
from Breezeway, things start getting worse

When you allow your neighborhood to go down
you have to pay the price
People lose respect for the community
You find very few individuals who are nice

We helped to keep things nice and clean
We had floor contests
The holidays were wonderful
But Christmas was the best

Our community was close-knit
We encouraged each other to press-on
We worked with those who wanted to quit

You couldn't ask for much more
We were the last of the dedicated families
who moved from Thirty-Five Seventeen in 1974
Stateway Gardens was born in 1958
15 years later, it lost its resiliency

It was primarily due to poor judgment
and lack of responsibility
It could have been the best residence
Where anyone could have stayed
Where you didn't have to be fenced-in
Where children could have safely played

Where drugs and gang activity
could have been deterred
Where there was basically respect for everyone and
you didn't consistently hear the forbidden word

Where security officers could have been straight
Where an ounce of care and humility
played the largest role and that one person
could have made a difference but now it is too late

I remember Stateway Gardens
When puppy love was just that.
When we played with our Mom's high-heel shoes
and our Father's ties and hats

When the girls loved a certain boy who was tall, dark
and handsome and he had no clue
When I secretly fell in love with Jackie Ray and I didn't
know what to say or do

I remember Stateway when I played tricks
on my favorite friends, writing love letters and
pretending they were from young men
I remember making prank calls pretending to be a boy
and rapping to the girls and hearing the joy

I remember Stateway when I had to reveal my
devilish secret to my surprised friends
and them telling me to watch my back
They got me back because they didn't forget

Stateway Gardens helped me to grow
I see so many success stories
More than you'll ever know

Some of our neighbors have moved on
relocating to a more peaceful place
Fond memories of them leave a smile upon my face
When I saw the very first building being torn down,
I felt a void, but my heart has reserved space.

Thirty-Five Seventeen was one of the first
buildings to be developed on Federal
Now it is simply a different place.

I realize that Stateway will be no more,
But developers have something in store.

I remember block parties
I remember the breezeway
I remember strength
I remember beauty
I remember joy
I remember love
I won't forget Stateway

The Crook-Ect Cop

He's an officer who appears to be perf*ect*.

He's sworn in to serve and prot*ect*. This is the

kind of criminal you would never susp*ect*. He

fails to give his superiors, partner, family and

friends resp*ect*. This is a situation that one

must carefully dissect. To follow professional

standards and ethics, he will neglect. He is the

type of person no one should ever rej*ect*. Once

you cross him he will never forg*et*. He will

commit corruption, extortion, brutality and

malicious acts when be begins to proj*ect*.

Circumstances should definitely be noted in

circumsp*ect*. A tainted cop represents the

entire force in retrosp*ect*. When I think about a

dedicated officer, it makes me refl*ect*. They do

deserve utmost honor and respect. We don't

exp*ect* a sworn officer to be crook-*ect*!

Death On-Call

You drive, walk, jog, and you take the bus.
You use your cell phone without a care or a fuss.

Now, Seriously speaking!
You can catch hell

You can do many things on your home phone
that you shouldn't do while outside on your cell

I simply need to make things clear to you
Please pardon me but I do need to mention that while
we are on the cell, we simply don't pay attention!

Before we know it, it is definitely too late
The cellular phone is known for a high death rate

The cell phone is known for getting a lot of liars and
cheaters into trouble
It not only sent people to jail, but has busted millions
of people's bubbles

It's not used with discretion
It's not used with much care

It should come with a consumer warning,
"Buyer Beware!"

Despite us disliking consumer restrictions,
many of us have cell-phone-addictions

Cell phones are responsible for road rage-"Driving
While Mad"

It is reportedly known for contributing to other things
that are simply bad

The cell phone can cause a lot of pain and they are
known to cause strife,
but they are also known to save a person's life

These are really expensive objects that people will lie
for
Unfortunately, these small toys are what people will
steal and die for

If it's really important to talk, use a hands-free headset
or just pull over
Your life is worth the wait!
Use other people's experiences as a lesson before it is
too late

This message is very important
and it should not be taken for granted at all
Life is so precious
Remember the warning,
"Death On-Call"

Star Obsession

The tabloids have a ball spying on and discrediting the stars.
Fanatics find it difficult to learn simple lessons.
They don't realize that they are known to have star obsessions.
They're the sly media in unmarked cars
and the groupies who are obsessed with chasing the stars.
It is the woman who makes it a point to go after the athlete.
She only wants to be associated with his money and end up in defeat.
It is the man with the flowers and candy who pretends to be faithful.
After a short period of romance, it becomes apparent that he is dangerously hateful.
Obsessed fans attract stars by appearing adorable.
They spend their last dime on things that are not affordable.
The unsuspecting star ends up mingling with the fan who commits forbidden acts.
Their hidden agendas become apparent
and they want to attack.
The information is not hard to understand or too difficult to sort.
Many stars and their fans end up dying or in court.
So many stars have had their fate determined by an obsessed or hateful fan.
A star does not have to be world renowned,
but it can be the average woman or man.
It is definitely important to be more observant and mature being in your kind of profession.
Don't have an obsessed or irate fan to teach you the wrong kind of lesson.

Homeless Tears

Without an address I am unable to obtain a job.
I want to earn a living so that I can eat.
I must eat from the trash can and wear your
unwanted shoes on my feet.

We have no home because I lost my job.
I lost all faith and hope when I lost my family.
I became an obnoxious slob.

My family now lives with friends in another state.
They promised to come back.
I wasn't successful in finding employment.
I fear now that it is too late.

How do I survive with no place to live?
How long do I beg when no one wants to give?

I had everything that any man could ask for.
I had the family, house, cars and even more.

I took for granted the wonderful people in my life.
I lost the house, cars, children and my wife.

I never dreamed of sleeping inside a cardboard
box.
I wear dirty clothes and no socks.

My hair is matted because I choose to use no comb.
I lost everything that I love, especially my home.

I now realize that material things can be taken away.
I had a chance at living responsibly but I chose to play.

I now know things that I didn't know. I think that it is because I was forced to grow.

I am here through the grace of God, despite being homeless.
I could be dead and gone, but I am a living witness.

I want to work. I want my family. I want a house and car.
I want to do what's right for me. I now realize where my priorities are.

But I am homeless and I look fretful.
Every time I try to pick myself up, others are dreadful.

There are millions of homeless people in the world today.

Some of us are homeless by choice and others by force.
I became homeless due to an illegal source.

Please realize that all homeless people are not the same.
I know that I have only myself to blame.

I am trying to redeem myself.
I want to confess.
I want to work, but how can I get a job without an address?

Son To Mother

Oh Mom!

These words are so hard to say.

I am unable to hold back the tears.

I saw you on the corner today.

You don't even know me but I do know you.

I really didn't want to believe it,

but the things people said were true.

I stood and watched you wiggle your body.

Why are you doing that?

Why did you leave us?

Why did you have me?

Why are men touching you and pushing you around?

Why did you abandon us never to be found?

Daddy remembers you.

He has been a great Dad.

He never married again.

Sometimes I wished he had.

He protected us from the things that only he could see.

He made us his sole responsibility.

The only females I've had were the teachers in my life.

They knew that I was a Motherless child

with a Father who had no wife.

They respected his privacy.

They took care of me.

They taught me very well and made me able to see

that I should still love you despite who you are.

You ran away from us but you didn't get very far.

I found you over fifty miles from where you ran away.

I can't talk to you, but I have so much to say.

You simply don't know the people in your life.

You don't remember being a brand new mother and

not even being a wife.

You choose to sell your body as if it were an object.

You'd rather be self-enslaved than to receive self-respect.

Has it ever occurred to you that those men are

Fathers who have children too?

Do you ever think that your circle of life is filled

with sexual exploitation?

Do you want to continue to tarnish your reputation?

Just imagine how others feel about your public

indecency.

After reading my note, will you listen to me?

Will you go and get help and live responsibly?

Life is so beautiful and it can work for you.

Just put your faith in the Lord and make your dreams

come true.

This note is not a joke.

It is not a senseless prank.

Feel what I have to say and make it a point to thank

the Lord for bringing me back into your life.

I'll never deny you being my Mother.

My Father denies having a wife.

I don't blame him for being that way.

One day I'll walk up to you and simply say:

I love you Mom.

I appreciate what you've done.

You heard my cry and took heed.

You heard my cry in my note.

Your Loving Son

Because It's Powerful!

It empowers us to sing a beautiful song
It makes happiness last a lifetime long
It motivates us to unselfishly give
It provides a place for us to comfortably live
It brings long-lost families back together
It introduces unity into cultures in any weather
It allows our hearts to be filled with pleasure
It provides keepsakes for us to appreciate and treasure
It conquers the hate that trickles through
It directs us to be deserving, worthwhile, and true
It disallows negative thoughts and insensitive questions
It teaches us positive and unblemished lessons
It safeguards us from hate and jealousy
It makes sure our hearts are filled spiritually
It allows us to see a precious life
It protects us from the pain and strife
It proliferates right through you
and makes sure you remain moral and true
It discourages you from asking, "Why?"
It encourages a man to let go and cry
It brings the dishonest person back on track
It puts the past behind without looking back
It makes a person open up and face reality
It provides a strong foundation abundantly
It is on time every second, minute and every hour
It is the greatest emotion with remarkable power!
It is created from the heaven above
God is our Father, Holy Spirit and God is Love!
It's never stated a negative word or thought
It commands us all not to give up when we want to quit
It's the umbrella that allows us to love
That's what love has to do with it!

The Emotional Baggage Handler

"I don't want to hear that shit anymore!
I've said what I've had to say. I mean it now.
Stop it! Leave the past just where it belongs,
damn it!"

The emotional *baggage handler* gets tangled in

dirty laundry that is hard to get rid of.

They unsuspectingly take in baggage and fall in

love.

The person who complains, protests, and

badgers, inflicts undeserved abuse.

The baggage handler arrives at the

understanding that the

relationship is no use.

The emotional bag lady or man brings

unresolved issues from their past.

They are obsessed with issues that are

Irrelevant.

They make the drama last.

73

Obsessions with past problems make the

baggage lady or man feels entirely right.

All they want to do is argue, complain and fight.

Bad baggage is people with issues that choose

to trip.

They imagine you with another person and then

they flip.

They accuse you of cheating with someone else.

But they're the ones who are really cheating

themselves.

They use vulgar language like "mother-fucker

and bitch"

They know only words and phrases that are

Stereotypic.

They say that they want to be pleased in a

certain way.

They only want you to listen to what

they have to say.

They want to fight when they get angry or mad.

When they are miserable, they punishably

want you sad.

We all come with baggage, some bad and some

good

Some of us don't know how to maintain our

laundry like we should.

Never make it a point to say bad things about

your ex.

Never make it a point to say how big you want a

penis or breasts.

Body parts are not made to order but they are

criticized by the baggage lady or man who

makes it a point to apprise.

Take it from a *baggage handler* who has

experienced it. Send the bad baggage back

where it came from. Get rid of the garbage.

Better yet, get rid of that shit!

Simultaneous

Be my eyes.

I'll be your ear.

I will be able to see.

You will be able to hear.

Be my legs.

I'll be your voice.

I'll be able to walk.

You'll be able to talk.

Be my shoulders.

I'll be your hand.

With your hand in mine,

we'll simultaneously stand.

Our strength enables us.

It also empowers us.

They are strengths

that are simultaneous.

Your Winning Day

To put forth effort are steps to achieving.
To follow your dreams, yourself, you must believe in.
This occasion is shared in a very special way.
You will leave but the mark you've made will stay.
This date has been set for your graduation. We wish
you the sincerest congratulations.
We often hear you say,
"I wish I had known!"
You've made mistakes and accomplishments.
You have certainly grown!
You are the adults of tomorrow.
There are paths that you must take.
You have a winning edge.
There are decisions that you must make.
You will think about your future and past experiences
from day to day.
With hard work and determination
you will be on your way.
Challenges, hard work and obstacles will definitely be.
When you encounter them,
maintain your faith, confidence
strength and integrity.
Some things must come to an end.
This is the first day of the rest of your life.
This is your beginning!
You have dreams that can last forever.
You are winning!
Make possible the credentials you endeavor.
Maintain focus and you will achieve.
To be a winner, in yourself, you must believe!

An Immeasurable Gift

This Christmas dedication is my gift,

especially to you, the hard workers who are

supportive, dedicated and true. Worlds of

secretaries are at the top of the list. They are

the hands to their bosses arms and wrists. I

would like to honor the ancillary personnel.

They execute their duties exceptionally well.

There are professionals who are absolutely

resourceful. They make others aware. No

matter your customer service needs, they'll

certainly be there. There are individuals who

landscape our environment and others who

keep it clean. Nutritionists prepare menus to

assist us in staying healthy and lean. There are so

many supportive individuals who make our world a

better place to live. Some of them volunteer and

unselfishly give. It is truly an honor and pleasure to

submit to you a gift that one could always treasure.

It Won't Hurt

Will it hurt us to simply say

"Good morning, good night,

good afternoon or good-bye?"

Can these courteous words be stated without

asking why?

We automatically say *ouch* when we feel some

type of pain.

Some of us will, at times, cry.

When we see each other for the first time each

day, can we greet each other automatically

without giving it a try?

Greetings should be automatic,

spontaneous and should be

executed anytime and any place.

Let's greet each other, even if it is just a

nod with a smile,

when we meet face to face.

A Resilient Woman

She keeps in mind her spiritual, physical, mental, financial and emotional strength and how they play a key role. She realizes that it's okay to feel good about herself while keeping in mind that others are equally important. She maintains her personal goal.

No matter how much people try to take away from her and strip her of, she maintains her respect, dignity and love. She is aware of a culturally diverse world and allows others their spiritual space. She reassesses herself. She realizes that it is herself that she must first face.

She is self-actualized. She is a woman of perseverance. Will you be able to take her being direct? Do you prefer to control her being and still require respect?

Will you try to date her and deceive her out of spite? Or will you be an intelligent man who's strong and does what is right?

She is a woman who strongly believes in integrity. Don't invade her personal space with the male philosophy.

Will it bother you when she defends her honor and tells you how she feels?
When she intelligently states to you what she would like to do, will you do what you will?

Do you dislike her strong convictions and her beliefs that a woman can stand on her own?
Will you be arrogant and criticize her instead of leaving her alone?

She will not invite you into her home for you to humiliate her intentionally.
Since you two have no ties and nothing else in common, will you accept this begrudgingly?

Will you choose to waste her time and try to prove a point?
Don't try to make her miserable because you resent her. Please don't!

Do you feel offended about my strength and resiliency?
Would you accept the woman I am?
Would you rather dismiss me at my expense and you shouldn't give a damn?

I'm not willing to accept arrogance, insecurity and a man's indiscretions.
If he wants to teach me, I prefer the positive lessons.

I am willing to listen. I am willing to learn.
When I share with you, my respect you must have earned.

I will offer myself to you as one who can help you make it.
When you witness my resiliency, that's when you can't take it.

The King With The Dream

He traveled throughout many states to protest
segregation
He despised racial violence which was an
aggravation
A civil rights leader was he who fought for every
race, religion and culture
He is uniquely special
Like him there is no other
So many troubled minds
caused him so much pain
Despite the terrible conditions,
he fought for us in the sun and rain
An irrational person misunderstood him
and took away his life
The King left us to mourn
loyal supporters, children and a beautiful wife
His dream was slightly shattered
It made it through many trying times
King's Dream lives on
He shared it and made it yours and mine
The world still continues to keep it strong
Our King's day has become a national holiday
It took blood, sweat and tears but the Lord made a
way
Our King made an impact on our lives
Many people thought that it would be an impossible
feat
Our King took charge
Our King was strong
Our King was brave
Most of all, he was discreet

My Quiet Storm

My quiet storm is aired from late evening
until early morn. It is soft sensual music and the
reading of poems.

It gives you joy when you've experienced pain. It
soothes you with melodic rain.

I am the lady who hosts "My Quiet Storm".
Call me and allow me to mesmerize you.
I am on radio station WPOET 102.

My guests are invited
to share their innermost feelings.
I feel what they have to say.

I'll be your mediator
who objectively shares from my heart.
I am a woman of compassion who plays an integral
part.

The Poet's station is where you can be you.
It shares so much with its listeners.
That's radio station P102.

The Day Bubble Gum Took My Breath Away

I was walking and being silly chewing bubble gum.

My friend even noticed me and asked me for some.

I blew a couple of bubbles and got some on my lips.

I popped it and pulled it with my fingertips.

I blew a big bubble that obstructed my vision.

OOPS!

I tripped over the curb.

I dropped my books and grabbed a light pole.

I swayed and I swerved.

My heart was pounding fast!

I hoped that this episode wouldn't last.

I took a deep breath and pulled the bubble back in.

I inhaled it too hard.

That's when my biggest trouble began!

For a few seconds I got excited, not knowing what to do.

If you don't think that gum can take your breath away,

I lost mine.

Believe me. It's true!

I picked up my books and straightened up my clothes.

I felt gum on my lips and at the tip of my nose.

I rubbed it off too hard and it really did hurt.

I should have used soap and water.

Instead, I used my shirt.

My friend stood in a state of shock.

He could not move an inch.

I called out to him and gave him a pinch.

We both laughed and joked for a while.

Walking, carrying books and chewing gum is not my style.

I used to think that wind could only take your breath away.

No matter what flavor, bubble gum can too.

If you can imagine this only happening to me,

walking and chewing bubble gum can be a difficult thing to do.

African-American History in The Making

African American History is eminent everyday

but is celebrated in the month of February in a very

special way.

It is a time to share talents, contributions, and much

more.

It signifies strength, unity and a world of success.

It encourages us to work and celebrate together.

It requires us to make a world of difference.

Let us not forget our historians, past, present and those

(children) of our future....

*H*istorians past, present, and future

*I*nspire

*S*tudents of all ages

*T*o

*O*rganize African American

*R*oots

*Y*ear-round

Life's an Egg!

Life's an egg.
First it's conceived and eventually delivered.

It goes through life's process.
Then it dissipates.

A cracked egg becomes confused and may eventually
be institutionalized.

Many of them are rolling around.
Be careful! They have unresolved issues.

A hard-boiled egg is stubborn and demanding.
It is sometimes insatiable.
It generally gets what it wants.

The soft-boiled egg is sometimes misunderstood.
People mistake it for a doormat.

It's sensitive and yet strong.
It can fool a lot of people.

The scrambled egg is indecisive and often unsure.
It can be fickle.

Once you think you have it,
it comes out of a bag.
It appears fine but it can be cold and bitter.

A poached egg is slick and can get by in most cases.
Watch it!

You're standing there talking
and it can have its hand in your pocket.

The over-easy egg is said to be cool, calm and
collected.

It can take on many challenges and maintain
strength.

The sunny-side-up egg is energetic and positive.
It can make many people happy.
It is very resilient.

The rotten egg is deceitful!
You never know what's going on with it until it's
exposed.
It can be conniving and corruptible.

Never be fooled by the appearance of an egg.
The outside can definitely fool you.

The best egg lesson is to use common sense and
discretion.

The Mirror Image

Look in the mirror and you will see
you're in no position to criticize me.

You're more concerned with what I've got.
I am humble, something you're not.

You say all the bad things you want to say
to try to deter me from being a certain way.

You disrespect God's great creatures,
who are total beings with uniquely different features.

Those are things you actively fail to admire.
A proper attitude is what you must acquire.

You tell me how I should think, dress, and act.
If you look into the mirror, it will provide the facts.

Imagine being outside looking into the sky.

As every single cloud has its shape and form, you have
character traits too.

I am a world of many different people possessing
different cultures.
It's unfair to ask me, "What or who are you?"

Your words are so condescending and you are totally
out of place.
Continue to look into the mirror and observe it face to
face.
As you concentrate on yourself, please realize and know
that self-assessment and acceptance allow you to grow.

Genealogical Differences

"A man who sings of love is caring, but a man
who speaks of love is displaying a sign of
weakness," so it is said.

A man who practices chivalry is considered to be
"Hen-pecked."
Who, but a man, developed the concepts?

Just as a woman feels pain, so does a man.
We, unfortunately, dictate how men and women
should feel when something has negatively
impacted their lives.

Since we are unable to feel the pain of others,
we are not in a position or authority to state
that women experience more pain than men or
women are more emotional than men.
Statistics will prove differently.

We are not in a position to say who brings more
baggage into a relationship since all baggage is
relative and is not all negative.

Every individual situation is uniquely different.
Instead of man and woman criticizing each
other and competing to see who does what
better or worse, they should respect each
other's differences.

In The Cradle of My Eyes

I speak of no pain but a mere tear that refuses
to fall, explains hidden feelings, and sits right in
the cradle of my eyes.

In the cradle of my eyes where a tear refuses to
fall, I witness men and women not getting along
at all.

I am a person who feels bad for society because
it dictates what people should and should not be
and what they should and should not do.

Society experiences problems also, because it's
simply made up of people like you and myself.

"Men are not supposed to cry. We are supposed
to be strong."
If we did everything that you dictated to us,
then men and women would never get along.

I was bitter, angry and mad. I listened to
others instead of the truth. My stereotypic
attitude makes the situation sad.

I did not treat women with respect because I
didn't know how.
I made many changes in my life.
I cherish all women now.

I want to be loved and I want to love also. Now
is the time that I choose to grow.

You don't compromise a person's worth and integrity. I wish there were more, but only a small percentage of people want to be treated with respect and enter into a relationship responsibly.

I witness us not getting along all across the world. The prejudice starts at home when we are little boys and girls.

We mainly believe in things that are strictly hearsay. Despite witnessing bad relationships, many of us would rather choose to play.

I feel remorse for the things that I have done to women, but I am unable to cry. When I did hurt a woman, she looked at me with sadness and asked me reasons why.

I told her that I love her, but she couldn't understand, because I treated her cruel. I had become a heartless man.

I realize now that when I am profoundly touched by something, I'll be filled with unexpected surprise.

A very special woman will touch me
and she'll help turn my life around.
I'll be strong and allow tears to flow from both my eyes.

The Insecure Man

An independent woman he will resent.
To emotionally depend on her, his time is well
spent.

When his preference is not academics, he's
inferior to a woman's education.
She has worked hard and has already gone
through much stress to get where she is.
But he wants her to live the way he lives.

He feels inadequate when she willingly shares
information.
He becomes intellectually pretentious to protect
his reputation.

He'll expect his woman to be faithful,
understanding and true,
while he makes his rounds with anyone he
wants to.

For him to have someone else is not unfair. But
you are a dirty woman to him
because where he's touched you, someone else
has touched you there.

His ego hurts!
He doesn't think that you should do what he can
do. He wants you all to himself.
He also wants to be unfaithful and uncommitted
to you.

"Double Standards" is his middle name.

He'll spitefully hurt a woman and prevent her
from doing the same.

Whether he is married or singe, he'll lie to get
what he can. Then he has successfully
succeeded in self-indulgence, he feels that he's
the man.

To share with someone else, he gives more to
himself. Definitely!
He'll drain a woman of her money, if he could,
and he'll give to her reluctantly.

When a woman experiences more than
enough injustice, she'll finally treat the insecure
man with caution.

He'll never give honest and committed love
because he's in his own little world.
While he's being treated well in every way
possible, he treats a woman like a little girl.

He'll close up while using a woman and taking
advantage of her all at the same time.
Let it happen to him.
He might commit a crime.

It is very unfortunate when the man you love is
ruined from being selfish and personal
corruption.

He's not worth a woman's time, and yet he feels
that she should be treated like other women
he's had in his life.
The insecure man is not only single,
but he is also one who has a wife!

Arrogant is he and insensitive to a woman's
needs.
Don't go to him for comforting or your heart will
bleed.

A woman wants to encourage and comfort him
and she wants to hear what he has to say.
He'll tell her that nothing is wrong, when it is,
and he'll push her away.

He's afraid to love.
It's been a problem for hundreds of years.
He'll lie to you, accuse you, abuse you,
and leave you with many fears.

He does wrong and feels that there's no need
for him to change. The insecure man is neurotic,
emotional and selfish.
He is, in one word, baggage!

The Insecure Woman

The insecure woman will fight a strong and beautiful woman whom she feels is a threat. She'll compromise her friendship and sleep with her best friend's man on a bet.

If she had to choose between a man and her children, he would come first. She'll abandon her children for drugs, sex, and the party life that makes matters worse.

She is physically attracted to any man she meets. She compromises her worth and seeks financial and emotional security on the streets.

She doesn't care if the man she has an interest in is with a wife. She will brag about stealing him and threaten the woman's life.

She'll dog-out another woman whom she feels threatened by. She'll curse out anyone without a reason why.

She'll frequent bars, sporting events, malls, and other social affairs. Disregarding social etiquette, it's her body that she shares.

She's an authority on everything that she wants you to hear. She'll shy away from self-assured individuals that she fears.

She'll have unprotected sex with any man who'll have her. With a lost identity, she'll seek out the man who is the nurturer.

She'll do anything for the love of prestige, money,

drugs or a man. She gives of herself, but it's herself that she doesn't understand.

She'll walk all over people by misrepresenting to get ahead. She'll prove her worthiness and abilities by sharing her bed.

She'll have a man who emotionally and physically abuses. It doesn't even matter if he is the kind of man that misuses.

If she becomes pregnant, she'll accommodate her man and have an abortion. She'll prove her commitment to him and even commit extortion.

She can be blinded by the penis and catch nothing but hell. Being Penis-whipped will result in her going to jail.

She'll talk about anybody that she faces.
She'll even invade other people's personal spaces.

She provides unsolicited and unwelcome information.
She never realizes her grossly offensive reputation.

She wants to fulfill a man's wildest and unimaginable dream. The insecure woman is simply a woman who is disrespectful and with low self-esteem.

A Woman Definitely Knows

A woman knows when you're doing wrong.
You make excuses and then leave home.

You call from work and say that you'll be late.
To be with your lover, you definitely can't wait.

You know not much about you lover's life.
You think that you know all about your girlfriend or wife.

You say you don't like it when she nags.
You make her look worthless, but on yourself you'll
brag.

You do what you want to because it feels right.
But deep down inside, with your conscience you fight.

You definitely love your woman, but it's your lover
you're afraid to lose.
You're given an ultimatum by one or both of them and
you ultimately become confused.

Now, you're accusing your woman of fooling around to
take the attention away from you.
Having another man in her life definitely isn't true.

You continue to sleep around and become more
careless.
You give her many reasons to become suspicious.

You act even more strangely and say that nothing is
wrong.
You give no justification as to why you stay from home.

You make your woman think that she's crazy, but she

knows better.
She understands much more than you think.
But you'd rather continue to mislead and confuse her.

Between events, your lover wants more from you.
You're in even deeper and you don't know what to do.

The situation is apparently in disarray.
Now you question if you still want to play.

If you're not faithful, loving and committed, you'll
definitely be alone.
Give to a woman the utmost respect and know that she
is strong.

Communicate objectively and listen to a woman.
Don't listen at her.
Hear what she has to say.

If she chooses to curtail the relationship, don't be
selfish knowing that you're not worth a woman's time.

It costs when people play.

There are many things in life that a person blows.

A relationship is one of them, because a woman
definitely knows.

ANNA MAE

An ambitious child who was full of energy despite being rejected by the people she trusted.
She kept them in her heart.

Never realizing that she would return to the people who had turned their backs on her, she loves them as much now as she did then. Each individual is intricately etched in her heart.

New to a town that changed her entire life, she was curious and yet apprehensive. She took chances and risks.

Abused by a man who gave her a new name, he deceived her, sexually abused her, and continuously disrespected her. He felt that because he made her, he could do what he will. She was already talented.

Making a decision in her life, she visits a friend who loved her like a sister. Her friend showed her how to be strong and brave by teaching Anna a significant chant. This changes her life.

After being more true to others than herself, suffering emotional/sexual abuse, being inflicted with countless beatings, and disrespected by the man she had children by, Anna picks up and runs. This was the first day of the rest of her life.

Eluding the man who was a pathological liar and neurotic, Anna makes a wise choice. She wants nothing but the name that was familiar to people, especially those who love and emulate her. She is the epitome of a success story.

"A Major Crush on a Beautiful Woman"

Forbidden by the rules of society, by morals of religion and personal doubt, there could be anything beautiful with so dark a secret, so flattering a thought though, of a man being impressed by a beautiful woman.

A beauty ever so unique never walked the face of the earth, body excellent in the eyes of any man. How could one capture the heart of such an intelligent and beautiful creature of God?

In the freedom of the forest, instincts and habits of the wild, which are constantly shunned, are brought out and rebirthed when such a woman is near. When such a woman is near, she can spark interests of such heat and passion that the forest is then ablaze.

Too bad, though, for the man who lives in a society where only friendship and morals should be allowed to take precedence over what one feels. But friendship can be just as satisfying and I have the advantage as long as you are near, to enjoy that which I may.

Then too, a mental affair, one of the expressions of ideas, thoughts and feelings of afar, doubts in my heart, and the triumphs I am bound to make, now really, that's a thought. Just maybe that's what counselors are for.

Respectfully submitted,

A student from St. Louis Job Corps-1988

"Juliette"

"Justice she seeks but she only finds denial

and criticism

Used, she feels, but she triumphantly

bounces back stronger than ever

Love she gives with no limits, but with

discretion

In her is a drive to be like no other

Each day she touches people with her

softness and caring heart

Today she looks toward the future

Tomorrow she makes it part of her every

existence

Enjoy life for it owes you so much because

you've given so much!"

Lydia

Fine Print

You know that you're the only one in my life
At least for now

I am married but I'm not with my wife
We sleep together when I visit the children

I'm seeing someone, but it's not serious
We just have sex

That's just a cold sore on my lip
I have one on my ass too

I always use protection
Only when I have a one-night stand

I don't like rejection
But I'll kick someone to the curb fast

The person you meet can be so sweet.
That's to impress you.
While you're opening up,
your new lover takes what you say
and uses it against you.

Unfortunately, you think that
your newfound friend is
just the person you're looking for.
You later find that they are only out to score.

When two people meet to establish a relationship,
one or both of them may actually be playing.

Carefully read between the lines
and hear what the person isn't saying.

Don't go on a tangent and misinterpret
what the person is saying.
When contradiction is apparent,
you know that the person is playing.

Playing is telling grandiose lies
for selfish gain and being dramatic without even trying.
Many failed relationships result in heartless
and jealous people conveniently lying.

They Choose Not To Grow

There are people who don't want to grow.
They don't want to know the things mature adults
should know.

They see it when you stare.
But they are immature.
Why should they care?

They don't have a heart.
They see the hurt they inflict.
They can tear people apart.

You can be at your best.
They will challenge you
and put you to the test.

They are children who are grown.
They choose not to know.
They elude reality.

They simply choose not to grow.
This is for innumerable reasons.
But they are not willing to let go.

Peoples-The Beautiful

We are all born with imperfections
We are children who seek protection

We are individuals born with different personalities

We must learn to respect other peoples' challenges and cultural diversities.

Why do we criticize each other and overlook our own discrepancies?

We look at others and tell them about their attitudes.

We fail to evaluate ourselves.
Some of us don't care to choose.

We talk about a person's accent, hair, skin color and some challenges that are visible to us.

When we are asked about ourselves, we simply choose not to discuss.

Some individuals relate better to negative things that people say.

The one, who severely judges, eludes criticism and will have it no other way.

There is conflict between families, friends, neighbors, politicians, and other countries with very little compromise.

There are too many people who are victims of jealously, hate and despise.

Is it not enough that we judge each other by socio-economic status, ability, culture and/or race?

When we are presented with mental pain, is it something that we care to face?

The biggest war is between the sexes and cultures for reasons that should never be.

Innocent victims are getting hurt and dying.
The victims are people of all nationalities.

It's absolutely wonderful that we all are unique in our very own and special way.

Can we promote racial harmony and commonwealth among all men today?

Peoples-The Beautiful it is imperative that we evaluate and assess our minds.

It's when we are prejudice, selfish, and harmful, we hide behind blinds.

It's Not Love

When one speaks of love and fails to apply it

When one wants others to love him but he refuses to

try it

When it is used selfishly and causes pain

When it is taken for granted and made powerless

When it is disrespected and used in vain

When one pretends it's love but has never loved before

When one plays with it and refuses to take it seriously

When one eludes it and chooses to ignore

When it is taken out of context and used for

unacceptable pleasures

When one puts on a facade and professes love

When one equates it with something else

and then tries to measure

When it is used as a secondary emotion

When it is not demonstrated in a genuine way

When a person holds it in and keeps it hidden until his

dying day

Caught-Up

You Just Can't

Continue to have a secret lover
without your mate being aware

Say I love you and be free of romance and care

Expect someone to stay with you
when you're being mean and disrespectful

Hide secrets when you know that
you are forgetful

Expect your mate to be faithful to you
when you have not relinquished your relation

Say that you are conditioned when you can't resist
temptation

Expect to have unprotected sex without being burned

Expect to have a beautiful relationship
when it hasn't been earned

Expect to make love and neglect the fact that
you can conceive a child

Expect to go through life without drawing a crowd

Fake Jewels

If you don't mean it, don't say it

If you're not genuine, don't pray it

If you're unable to afford it, don't take it

If you're different from others you admire, don't fake it

If you don't know it, don't try to speak it

If it's trouble you can't get into,

don't try to seek it

When you attain strength, don't lose it

When it's against your health, don't choose it

If you forbid others, don't you do it

When you reach your goal, stick to it

When you don't use appropriate life tools,

You lose perception and become fake jewels

His Best Friend

Someone told someone.
Then someone told you.
Now she's telling you that you are through.

He holds tears in the cradle of his eyes
His best friend told his girlfriend outrageous lies

He stands outside staring at the rain from above
He's distraught because he lost her love

He'll miss her

He really did care

Whenever she needed him, he made every effort to be
there

Someone told you something that really wasn't
true

He found out that his best friend really wanted
you

You left your love

His heart throbs with pain

He trusted his best friend

Both of you are the ones to blame

With My Eyes Closed

With my eyes closed,
You simply can't imagine what I am thinking
I wonder how can others witness what you fail
to see
I have discovered that you never took the
opportunity to get to know the original me
You have no idea what or how I feel
You want your ego caressed
You want to do what you will
What I want from you, others care to give
You want the benefits of life, but you're afraid to
live
You're only concerned when you see me staring
You ask me what's on my mind
Your self-absorption makes you uninformed
You selfishly become blind
With my eyes closed
I am imagining that I want no one else
I want the tender, caring and romantic
you
I want you to want me for the right reasons
I have priceless love that you can treasure
You can never name a second I've hurt you
It is genuine love that you don't have to
question
It is the kind of ingredient that you can never
measure
If I am dreaming, please let it come true
I don't want to dream with my eyes closed
I want to be right here with the tender and
trusting you

Take Me The Way I Am

If it is my attitude that is negative, then you
have every right to get rid of me

I would never impose upon you to accept my
contaminated personality

It is my physical attributes that I choose to
mention

I am not wearing revealing clothes to attract
your attention

I can validate being a woman without looking
for a super star

I've accepted your imperfections
I love you the way you are

The clothes I wear should do
My hair is virgin and it should be accepted too

I have some visible scars here and there

You have a down-to-earth woman in your life
and you are simply not aware

No living being is perfect
This is something that you should already know

If you see a woman that you think is the bomb,
you turn around and go

You promised to be a man once before

You tell your friends that you've made another score

It's time that I tell you just where you stand

Your boyish attitude has caused hardship
It has gotten out of hand

I am flesh and blood and not a material possession

It's when someone affects you and you learn your lesson

The first things you and your sexually excited friends see are my big breasts and ass

I am a woman with a brain and I certainly have class

You choose not to see me for yourself
You would rather imagine

Open your mind's eyes and see me
Take me the way I am and not what I am said to be

Play Me a Word Game

This is an activity without a name
It's simply an intriguing and provocative word
game

It has no rules
It has no instructions

It has no hard directions
It requires no education

It requires no particular race or culture
It teaches no concrete lessons

It can shift in conversation
It can change its mind

It does not require you to be perfect
It won't penalize you when you're unkind

It has no feelings
It inflicts no pain

It has nothing to give
It has nothing to gain

It can misspell itself
and use poor grammar

but it gets its point across

It makes no demands
but it shows you who's the boss

It is a game that can allow you to win
if it is played right

If you chose to play by your own rules,
it makes you lose sight

It makes you think that you are always flawless
in everything you say and do

This powerful word game plays tricks
and it plays vicious tricks on you

Your mind becomes victim to the words that you
simply say

Now you are disagreeing with how other people
play

You've been thinking that you were playing the
game and cheating on someone else,
but it's yourself that's been played, definitely

If you want to win, you must play fairly,
carefully and discreetly

No Intimation

You had no clue that the money you handled
was in the hands of a killer

That person that you criticized
was a world-known star

That ride you took
was my Father's car

That person you had beaten
was your best friend's brother

That lady that you cursed
was my Mother

The people that accepted you
have left you alone

You've struggled
with your conscience

You have no clue
how to distinguish
right from wrong

The Unblemished Man

Dearest Love,

Our hearts were in search of someone to belong
When we met, we both were attracted to each other
This feeling was so strong

We both told each other of our past and we made
known our intentions
We talked about what we wanted out of life, to
mention

It amazed me to experience a love I have accepted
totally
Unlike you, no other man was able to see that I was
genuine
I have you, a man who chooses to be monogamous
I feel your tenderness
This is exclusive love that was made for us

The day we make love our hearts will merge with your
body close to mine

I seek no other love
The love you display is very hard to find

I love you fully
I have never loved any man the way I love you
You are so special to me
You asked for a chance to prove your love for me
You know how to treat me and you know exactly what
to do

You have made me happy
You long to place your tongue down my back
and massage me with your fingertips
You want to rock me steady while holding my wavy
hips

I allowed you to kiss me and I am quite pleased
You move your body gently and you do it with ease

I want you to rain down on me while I am under
I want you to hit me with a powerful thunder

I appreciate your respect, genuineness, and caress

It is time to strike lightning together
Allow me to take over now because it's your body that
I want to bless

I want you to counteract and make me shake
Be like fireworks that sound like an earthquake

Let our love be the chain that is unable to be broken
Let our words together be the only sensual words that
are spoken

We no longer have to search for a person to belong
You love the woman I am
I am grateful to have the perfect man of my own

PS

As I sit and write this letter, I am in need of someone
to belong. It feels good to know that I can simply
dream and write about the unblemished man of my
own.

My Affectionate Moon

She's a glowing and natural element that generates love

Affectionate Moon holds a lot of devotion in the cradle of her heart

She experiences a lot of atmospheric pressure, but she endures environmental stress

A small percentage of people know how to treat her because she is mysterious and certainly misunderstood

She's obedient

Many have walked on the Moon, but she remains gentle and treats people like she should

Her surface is only lined with tenderness from within

Family, lovers and even friends have mistreated her affectionate nature

She's been told that she's too kind
Individuals with motives and hidden agendas are in disbelief

They take her kindness for weakness

She maintains strength after a few moments of temporary grief

The Moon has a complicated nature but she makes things easy for you

She'll shield herself from the bad elements

She detects confusion and realizes what she must do

She'll continue to rotate like nothing has happened and make you think that she's not aware

She'll treat you accordingly and continue to display care

She'll let you know as much as she pleases

She has a way with words that she literally teases

She doesn't play mind games that will make a person feel incompetent

When she realizes that someone has been affected by her profound thoughts,
she apologizes and provides solace

Affectionately supporting mankind is her genuine commitment

My Love On Valentine's Day

On February 14TH

with you my love

Little Cupid's up above

When you come to the door

I'll be there just like before

There is something

you should not miss,

a big beautiful Valentine's kiss

I will kiss you

I will hold you tight

I will be romantic

with all of my might

I don't care if Cupid's arrow

is fast or slow

He only knows where it will go

Little Cupid's up above

On Valentine's Day with my Love

That Special Moment Endured

As your special moment approaches
Answer, "I do"
Take your hearts into each other's hands
Nothing shall come between you
When you take each other's hand
you'll know that she's yours and you're hers
During your special moment feel the love
you have never felt before
Touch each other's hearts
with words no one else has ever heard
Light up each other's lives with an endless smile
You will always be a radiant pair
Reach for stars together
There's nothing too good for you
Cherish the love you have for each other
Your special moment will last
Clear and positive thinking will work when you
work together
Your special moment will encompass occasional
obstacles
It was made to withstand any weather

Christmas With My Sensual Love

On this snowy day with my sensual love, there

are shimmering stars in the dark skies above

When you try to surprise me at the door

I'll be there just like before

Above our heads there will be

something special for us to see

I'll pretend that I don't know

You'll remind me of the mistletoe

You'll make sure that I don't miss

a big beautiful Christmas kiss

We can sit and sip to a toast

You will give me the gift I like the most

We can sit and watch snowflakes fall

We can pamper and bathe each other

and relax our minds most of all

With all the shiny stars above, I am spending

Christmas with my sensual love

The Man of Only My Dreams

I dreamed of him asking me how was my day.
I kissed him first before I would say.

I could clearly see that he was a gentleman and
he was fine.
I dreamed that he held me tight.
He was delighted that I made him mine.

I dreamed of him making passionate love to me
until both our hearts would pause.
I dreamed of him giving me candy. I had
flowers just because.

I appreciated his wonderful notes and thoughtful
gifts.
I recall him giving my lonely heart a lift.

He made everyday for me a thrill.
He made sure his love was something
that only I could feel.

I dreamed of you saying that I was the only one
for you.
I remember me telling you the same thing too.
I dreamed of a love that was made distinctively
for us two.

This poem is written for the man of only my
dreams. "You made me very happy because
you made it possible for my dreams to come
true."

A Call Of Fate

We met by chance
I had dialed the wrong number, of course

When I asked to speak to someone else,
he fell in love with my voice

This was a call I had to decline
I immediately put down the receiver
He immediately pressed star sixty-nine

I reluctantly talked
but this was a call too good to be true

Fate brought me back to a gentleman
whom I had a crush on for 25 years
and fate sent him back to someone he respectfully
knew

We both had someone else and neither of us dreamed
of ever seeing each other again

A wrong number can reunite a deserving woman and
man

A Seductive Birthday Gift

For your birthday
you can have me

I'll be the sweetest gift you ever did behold

This gift is a secret
It should not be told

Out of all the gifts you will receive
I'll be the gift that will actually tease

The other gifts can sit neatly on the shelf

You must open this gift slowly
so that it can reveal itself

Hold it close to you and see what you'll get

You'll open it dry but you'll come out wet
Enjoy the feel of the gift

Hear what it has to say
Enjoy this sensual gift for your birthday

When You Become Old

Remember when you called the elderly old?

When you didn't have a heart and stole
When you sold drugs for the sex and cash
When you went downtown and looked for
windows to smash

When you called your children stupid
and other bad names
When you did terrible things and looked for
others to blame

When you become old,
Will your teeth be filled with gold?

Will you accept being gray?
Stand on the corner to drink
and have unkind words to say
Have breasts filled with artificial fluid
Will you undress in the vehicle and still do it?

When you become old, will you have the same-
sex preference?

Will you sleep with multiple mates and continue
to go out on many dates?
Will race or culture make a difference?
Will you continue to do drive-bys
and use street drugs to get high?

Remember when you mugged people,
especially the elderly?

When you become old and someone mugs you,
Will you want to shoot?

Stand on the corner and still prostitute
Continue to be a drag queen
Have group sex like irresponsible teens

When you are old,
Will you be concerned about communicable
diseases?

Have a relationship with anyone who pleases
Will you look back and see how you
abused and neglected your kids?
Remember when you pimped a lot of women
and bragged about what you did?

When you pretended to be a Christian
and hid behind God
When you desperately wanted something
and you put on a facade

When you are old,
will you continue to commit adultery?

Continue to get off on pornography
Will you try to rap and forget what to say?
Will you remember from day-to-day?
Will you look back and see the pain you have
inflicted?
Will you remember how you
stole robbed, killed and became addicted?

When you become old, will you continue to
booty-shake and grind on the dance floor?

Will you continue to be promiscuous
but call a woman "whore?"
Produce explicit lyrics that make money from
words that exclusively disrespect
Have grandchildren like the kids you chose to
desert and neglect

When you become old, will you be able to face
yourself in the mirror and realize that it is a
blessing to age and see that the elderly helped
to build this world for you and me?

When you become old, can you grow old
gracefully and responsibly with dignity and
integrity?

Until He Saw Me

We met by chance
It was a phone call

I dialed the wrong number
I wasn't thinking at all

He answered the phone
I was expecting someone else, of course
When I apologized for dialing the wrong
number, he fell in love with my voice

I wasn't really interested in
What he had to say
I just listened to his happiness
I let him have his way

It was a meeting made by pure fate
Before I knew it, he asked me for a date

I was rather surprised
I had to immediately decline
When I put down the receiver, he pressed star
sixty-nine

I said hello
I didn't think it was he
He felt so touched and just wanted to speak
with me

I just wanted to be to myself
I wanted to go
He asked me my name

He needed to know

I told him my name
He waited to tell me his
He hesitated at first
Then he told me it was Kriz

I found it to be very strange,
the dialogue that we had
I wanted to hang up again
But I didn't want to make him mad

Kriz apologized for being so forward
To simply have perfect dialogue,
the whole situation seemed so sorted

I told him that I understand
I just wanted to know why he insisted on
talking to me
He said that he noticed my lovely voice
and he wanted to meet me

Before we decided on our first date
We talked on the phone for at least three
months and for many hours
Kriz sent me candy, perfume, stuffed animals
and expensive flowers

He enjoyed the things I had to say
Our personalities were a perfect match
We even shared the same birthday

The big day came
We talked minutes before our date
It was time for us to finally meet
Kriz told me that he could hardly wait

I was neutral about the matter
It seemed like fun
We met in busy downtown
I imagined, "Could this be the one?"

When I finally met Kriz
He had a horrible look on his face
Despite me looking exquisite,
I realized that he didn't accept my race

He shook my hand, instead of giving me a hug
When I reached out to him, he gave me a shrug

I realized we were not the same color
I was impressed with his background
He was impressed with my voice, a simple
human sound

Kriz had fallen in love with my voice
despite being well educated
He fell in love with imagination
He was foolishly infatuated

Kriz's education didn't matter
It didn't matter if he was a scholar in school
because he was prejudiced
I experienced an encounter with an educated
fool

Kriz loved everything about me before we met
He loved what he didn't see
He was seriously talking about love
That is.... until he saw me

A Perfect Home Wrecker

She is the woman who cares nothing about her
husband. He is the man who cares nothing for his
wife.
They are individuals who affect their own family
structure, especially the innocent child's life.

The children are made victims. They are hurt by it all.
The home wrecker uses poor discretion and makes
careless calls.

A perfect home wrecker will leave evidence visible.
They deny doing anything wrong. They'll lie for people
they were talking to on the telephone.

He thought he wanted to be a husband. She was never
meant to be a wife. A perfect home wrecker makes
excuses to commit fornication while destroying their
own mate's reputation.

The wife says that her husband doesn't know how to
satisfy her and he doesn't know how to keep a decent
job. The husband says that his wife is no longer
attractive to him and that she is a slob.

The poor children hear the fussing, fighting and tension
between their mom and dad. The children are robbed
of a decent family structure. They lack hope and love
because they are very sad.

A perfect home wrecker is not the one who comes
between the husband and wife.
The home wrecker is the one who promises to love,

honor, cherish, and be there for life.

A perfect home wrecker destroys the marriage and family and encourages a break-up anyway.
The husband and wife become angry and bitter about many things and they have repulsive things to say.

A perfect home wrecker could be the husband and it could even be the wife. Yes. It could be one or both of them who can destroy the family's life.

Keep in mind that a person does not steal a husband nor do they steal the wife. But they do contribute to a relationship that goes through pain and strife.